OPTIONS TRADING

Basics

A Beginner's Guide to Understanding Options

By

Michael J. Defosse

MS, MBA

Dedication

To the Whitman School of Management at Syracuse University

Suos Cultores Scientia Coronat

About the Author

Michael J. Defosse is a highly regarded finance professional with over 30 years of experience in securities trading, investment management, and risk management. He is the CEO of GlobEx Markets Ltd and the Managing Director of Market Savvy Investor LLC, where he leads with a wealth of knowledge and expertise gained from his extensive career.

Michael graduated from Syracuse University with a BA in Economics, an MS in Finance, and an MBA. Throughout his career, he has held prestigious positions at several top investment firms and risk management companies, establishing himself as a respected authority in the field.

As the author of the "Language of Global Finance" series and numerous instructional books and guides on personal finance, investing and investment strategies, Michael has made significant contributions to financial literature. His works are known for their clarity, accessibility, and actionable insights.

An avid traveler, Michael is also a passionate advocate for financial literacy. His journey into trading began as a stockbroker, just months before the market crash of 1987. Amassing knowledge through his years of personal and professional experiences, he now shares this expertise to educate and empower others. He is dedicated to demystifying the world of finance and helping individuals achieve financial independence through smart investment practices.

Michael lives in the Financial District of New York City, where he continues to influence and inspire the next generation of investors.

Preface

In the ever-evolving world of finance, many individuals find themselves overwhelmed by the complexities of investing. As an advocate for financial literacy, I have witnessed countless people making avoidable mistakes in their approach to investing and risk management. This observation, coupled with the volatility in financial markets and a high interest rate environment that sends mixed signals about the future, has driven me to share my experience and knowledge to help others navigate the often turbulent waters of the options trading.

My journey into trading began in 1987, prior to the market crash, which sparked a greater interest and passion for understanding and mastering financial strategies. Over the past several decades, I have honed my expertise in trading, investment management, and risk management, holding prestigious positions at top investment firms and risk management companies. This extensive background has provided me with a wealth of experience and practical knowledge that can benefit the next generation of investors.

"Options Trading Basics: A Beginner's Guide to Understanding Options." is a culmination of my efforts to demystify the basics of options trading. Options are powerful financial instruments that, when used correctly, can enhance investment portfolios through leverage, risk management, and strategic flexibility. However, the complexity of options also means they can lead to significant losses if not fully understood.

Throughout this book, I will guide you through the fundamentals, providing step-by-step guidance, practical examples, and an understanding of the factors that influence option pricing. You will learn how to better understand option contracts, choose appropriate strike prices and expiration dates, and execute basic trading strategies. Additionally, I will explore the benefits and potential risks associated with options trading, ensuring you are well-equipped to make informed decisions and avoid common pitfalls.

This is the first in a series of mini-books that I am publishing to help novice and inexperienced investors that are looking to refine and enhance their skills. Each book will be dedicated to a specific strategy or skill that covers the fundamental principles, practical application, and advanced techniques to enhance your trading acumen.

My mission is to empower you with the knowledge and confidence to take control of your financial future. By understanding the tools and implementing the strategies outlined in this book and my other books on investing, you can better manage risk, profit from volatility, and enhance your overall investment returns. Whether you are new to options trading or looking for a refresher on the fundamentals, this guide will serve as a valuable resource on your journey to financial success.

Thank you for embarking on this journey with me. Together, let's unlock the potential of your portfolio and embrace a smarter way to invest and generate income.

Michael J. Defosse, MS, MBA

CEO, GlobEx Markets LTD
Managing Director, Market Savvy Investor LLC

Contents

Introduction

Welcome to "Options Trading Basics: A Beginner's Guide to Understanding Options." This book is designed to take you on a journey from understanding the fundamental concepts of options trading to applying basic strategies effectively. Whether you are new to trading options or looking to enhance your investment skills, this guide will provide you with the necessary knowledge and tools to navigate the options market confidently.

In the first chapter, "Understanding Options," we delve into the core principles of what an options contract is, the types of options available, and essential terms and concepts. You'll learn about the underlying asset, strike price, expiration date, premium, contract size, and the critical differences between American and European options. This foundational knowledge will set the stage for your options trading journey.

Chapter 2, "How Options Work," explains the mechanics of options trading. You'll explore how options are traded, understand option chains, and discover the various factors that influence option prices. This chapter will equip you with the practical skills needed to analyze and execute options trades effectively.

In Chapter 3, "Basic Options Strategies," we introduce you to fundamental strategies such as buying call options and buying put options. You'll learn when to use these strategies, their potential benefits, and the associated risks. These basic strategies will form the cornerstone of your options trading toolkit.

Chapter 4, "Benefits and Risks in Options Trading," highlights the advantages of using options, such as leverage, flexibility, and risk management, while also addressing the inherent risks, including complexity and potential losses. This chapter aims to provide a balanced perspective on options trading, helping you make informed decisions.

Finally, Chapter 5, "Practical Tips for Successful Options Trading," offers valuable insights into setting up a trading plan, avoiding common mistakes, and learning from unsuccessful trades. This chapter emphasizes the importance of discipline, preparation, and continuous learning in achieving long-term success in options trading.

Why Learn Options Trading?

Learning options trading can significantly enhance your investment capabilities and open up new opportunities for profit and risk management. Unlike traditional stock trading, options provide a versatile toolset that allows you to leverage positions, hedge against potential losses, and generate additional income through various strategies. By understanding how options work, you can develop strategies to capitalize on market movements, regardless of whether the market is rising, falling, or remaining flat.

Moreover, in today's unpredictable economic environment, having a comprehensive understanding of options trading can provide you with a competitive edge. It empowers you to make more sophisticated investment decisions, better manage your portfolio, and protect your investments from adverse market conditions. Options trading is not just for professional traders; it is a valuable skill for any investor looking to improve their trading knowledge and financial literacy.

Now, let's embark on this journey together, starting with the basics of understanding options in Chapter 1.

Understanding Options

What is an Options Contract

An options contract is a financial agreement between two parties that gives the buyer the right, but not the obligation, to buy or sell an underlying asset at a predetermined price, known as the strike price, within a specified period. The underlying asset can be stocks, indices, commodities, or currencies. The seller of the options contract is obligated to fulfill the terms of the contract if the buyer decides to exercise their right. For this right, the buyer pays a premium to the seller. Options are versatile financial instruments that can be used for hedging, speculation, or generating income.

Types of Options

Call Option

A call option grants the holder the right, but not the obligation, to purchase a specified quantity of an underlying asset at a predetermined price up to the expiration date. The buyer pays a premium to the seller (or writer) of the option for this right.

One of the key benefits of a call option is that it offers limited risk to the buyer, as the maximum potential loss is restricted to the premium paid for the option. On the other hand, there is the potential for profit if the price of the underlying asset rises.

For example, if you buy a call option (long call) with a strike price of $50 on a stock currently trading at $45, you are speculating that the stock's price will rise above $50 before the expiration date. If the stock price exceeds $50, you can exercise your option to buy the stock at $50, potentially profiting from the difference minus the premium paid. You could also sell the call option at a profit instead of exercising the option.

The following illustration is the profit/loss chart for our long call option example, assuming a total premium of $100.

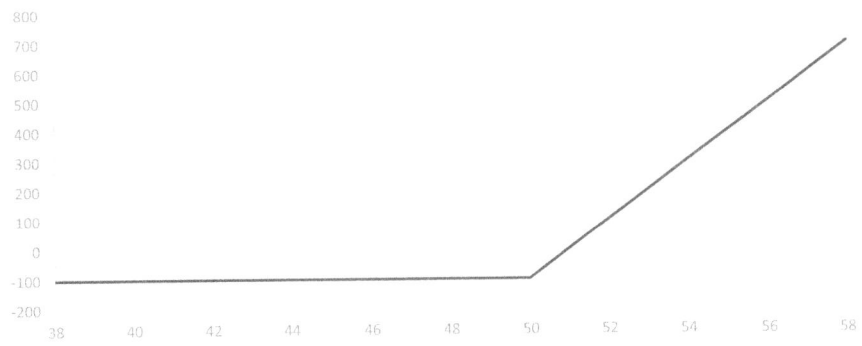

Source: MacrOptions

Put Option

A put option grants the holder the right, but not the obligation, to sell a specified quantity of an underlying asset at a predetermined price up to the expiration date. The buyer of the put option pays a premium to the seller (or writer) of the option for this right.

One of the main advantages of a put option is that it offers limited risk to the buyer, as the maximum potential loss is restricted to the premium paid for the option. On the other hand, there is the potential for profit if the price of the underlying asset decreases.

For example, if you buy a put option (long put) with a strike price of $50 on a stock currently trading at $55, you are speculating that the stock's price will fall below $50 before the expiration date. If the stock price drops to $45, you can exercise your option to sell the stock at $50, profiting from the difference minus the premium paid. You could also sell the put option at a profit instead of exercising the option.

The following illustration is the profit/loss chart for our long put option example, assuming a total premium of $100.

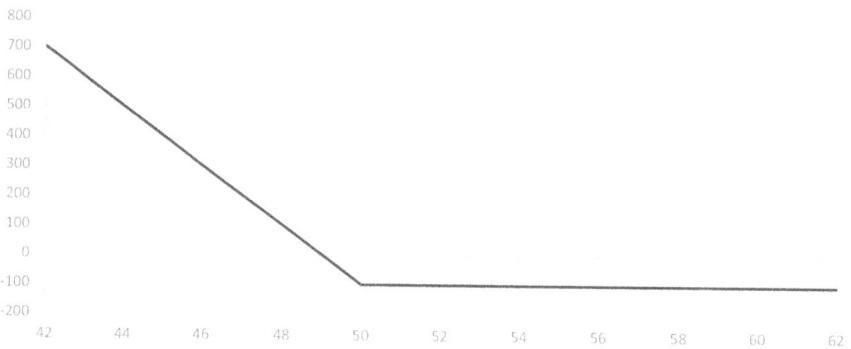

Source: MacrOptions

Basic Option Terms and Concepts

Underlying Asset

The underlying asset is the financial instrument on which an options contract is based, and it can take various forms such as a stock, an index, a commodity, or a currency. The value of the option is directly influenced by the price movements of this underlying asset. For instance, in a stock option, the underlying asset would be the specific stock to which the option pertains, and fluctuations in the stock's price will impact the option's value.

Similarly, options based on indices like the S&P 500, commodities such as gold or oil, or currency pairs like EUR/USD derive their value from the price movements of these underlying assets. Understanding the behavior and characteristics of the underlying asset is important, as it has an impact on the option's value and potential profitability.

Strike Price

The strike price, or exercise price, is the predetermined price at which the holder of an options contract can buy or sell the underlying asset. For a call option, the strike price is the price at which the holder can purchase the underlying asset. Conversely, for a put option, the strike price is the price at which the holder can sell the underlying asset. This price is established when the options contract is created and remains fixed throughout the life of the option.

The strike price is a crucial component of the options contract, as it determines the level at which the holder can exercise their rights and significantly impacts the option's intrinsic value and potential profitability. Understanding the strike price helps traders evaluate the potential outcomes of their options strategies.

Expiration Date

The expiration date, or maturity date, is the deadline by which an options contract must be exercised. If the option is not exercised by this date, it expires and becomes worthless. This date is critical in options trading as it defines the timeframe within which the holder can exercise their right to buy or sell the underlying asset.

Options can have various expiration cycles, such as monthly, weekly, or quarterly, allowing traders to choose a timeframe that aligns with their investment strategy. Understanding the expiration date is essential because it affects the option's value and the urgency of trading decisions. As the expiration date approaches, the option's time value decreases, impacting its overall price.

Premium

The premium is the price paid by the buyer to the seller (writer) for acquiring an options contract. It represents the cost of obtaining the right to buy (in the case of a call option) or sell (in the case of a put option) the underlying asset at the specified strike price before the option's expiration date.

Several factors influence the premium, including the current price of the underlying asset, the strike price, the time remaining until expiration, and market volatility. Higher volatility typically increases the premium due to the greater chance of significant price movements. The premium is a crucial component in options trading, determining the initial investment required and impacting potential profitability.

Contract Size

The contract size is the amount of the underlying asset that an options contract represents, with one standard stock options contract typically covering 100 shares of the underlying stock. This means that buying or selling a single options contract gives you the right to 100 shares, significantly amplifying your investment scale and potential exposure.

For example, purchasing one call option contract for a stock trading at $50 per share means you control 100 shares worth $5,000 in total. Similarly, writing one put option contract commits you to potentially buying 100 shares at the strike price if exercised.

Exercise

Exercise is the act of utilizing the right granted by an options contract, allowing the owner to buy (in the case of a call option) or sell (in the case of a put option) the underlying security at the predetermined strike price on or before the expiration date. When the owner claims this right and takes a long or short position in the underlying security, it is known as exercising the option.

Exercising is a crucial aspect of options trading, enabling the holder to capitalize on favorable market conditions as specified in the contract terms. Understanding the process and implications of exercising helps traders to effectively manage their positions.

Assignment

Assignment occurs when the seller of a call or put option is obligated to fulfill the terms of the contract. For a call option, the seller must sell the underlying stock, and for a put option, the seller must buy the underlying stock.

In every options trade, there are two parties involved: a buyer and a seller. When an option holder exercises their option, the seller on the other side of the trade is assigned and must complete the transaction as per the contract terms. Understanding assignment is crucial for options traders, as it represents the obligation they may face when writing options contracts.

Exercise Style: American Options vs European Options

- **American Options:** American options provide the holder with the flexibility to exercise the option at any time up to and including the expiration date. This feature allows the holder to capitalize on favorable price movements in the underlying asset whenever they occur during the life of the option.

  For example, if an investor holds an American call option and the underlying stock price rises significantly before the expiration date, they can choose to exercise the option early to capture the gain. This flexibility is particularly advantageous in volatile markets where prices can change rapidly, offering more opportunities for profit.

- **European Options**: European options can only be exercised on the expiration date, requiring the holder to wait until that specified date regardless of favorable market conditions beforehand. While this may seem like a limitation compared to American options, European options are often simpler to price and manage due to the fixed exercise date.

  Investors using European options must carefully plan their strategies, considering that they cannot act on short-term price movements and must rely on their predictions for the asset's price at expiration. This requires a well-thought-out approach, focusing on long-term market trends rather than short-term fluctuations.

Intrinsic Value

Intrinsic value is the amount by which an option is in-the-money (ITM). For a call option, it is the difference between the underlying asset's current price and the option's strike price, when the current price is higher. For a put option, it is the difference between the strike price and the underlying asset's current price, when the current price is lower. If this value is negative or zero, the intrinsic value is considered zero. Essentially, intrinsic value represents the real, immediate value of an option if it were exercised at the current moment.

Extrinsic Value

Extrinsic value, also known as time value, is the portion of an option's premium that exceeds its intrinsic value. It reflects the additional amount paid for the potential that the option's value may increase before expiration. This value is influenced by factors such as the time remaining until expiration, the volatility of the underlying asset, and prevailing market conditions. As the expiration date approaches, the extrinsic value diminishes, a phenomenon known as time decay.

Implied Volatility

Implied volatility measures the market's expectations for the future volatility of the underlying asset, derived from current options prices. It indicates how much the market believes the asset's price will fluctuate over the life of the option.

Higher implied volatility suggests that the market anticipates larger price swings, which typically increases the option's premium. Conversely, lower implied volatility indicates expectations of smaller price movements, resulting in a lower premium. Implied volatility is important for options traders, as it helps gauge market sentiment and assess the potential risk and reward of an options trade.

Open Interest

Open interest is the total number of outstanding options contracts for a specific strike price and expiration date that have not been settled or closed.

It represents the number of active positions in the market, indicating the liquidity and activity level of that particular options contract.

High open interest suggests many traders are involved in the contract, making it easier to enter and exit positions. Conversely, low open interest indicates fewer participants, which can lead to wider bid-ask spreads and less favorable trading conditions. Understanding open interest helps options traders assess market participation.

Bid-Ask Spread

The bid-ask spread is the difference between the highest price a buyer is willing to pay for an option (the bid) and the lowest price a seller is willing to accept (the ask). It represents the transaction cost for trading the option.

A narrow bid-ask spread indicates high liquidity and active trading, making it easier and more cost-effective to buy or sell the option. Conversely, a wide bid-ask spread suggests lower liquidity and higher transaction costs, as there is a larger gap between what buyers and sellers are willing to accept. Understanding the bid-ask spread helps traders evaluate the trading efficiency and potential costs of entering or exiting an options position.

Underlying Price

The underlying price is the current market price of the asset on which an options contract is based, such as a stock, index, commodity, or currency. This price is a critical factor in determining the value of an options contract, influencing both its intrinsic and extrinsic values.

For example, the closer the underlying price is to the strike price, the more likely the option will be in-the-money, affecting its overall premium. Understanding the underlying price helps options traders make informed decisions about when to buy or sell options based on their expectations of future price movements.

Greeks

The Greeks are a set of risk measurements that help options traders understand how different factors affect the price of an options contract. Each Greek measures the sensitivity of the option's price to various elements, such as changes in the underlying asset's price, time decay, volatility, and interest rates. The primary Greeks that most options traders focus on include:

- **Delta:** Measures the sensitivity of the option's price to a $1 change in the underlying asset's price.

- **Gamma:** Measures the rate of change of delta for a $1 change in the underlying asset's price.

- **Theta:** Measures the sensitivity of the option's price to the passage of time, also known as time decay.

- **Vega:** Measures the sensitivity of the option's price to changes in the volatility of the underlying asset.

- **Rho:** Measures the sensitivity of the option's price to changes in interest rates.

7 Key Characteristics of Options

Options are versatile financial instruments with several key characteristics that are important for investors and traders to understand:

Right to Buy or Sell

Options give the holder the right, but not the obligation, to buy (in the case of a call option) or sell (in the case of a put option) an underlying asset at a predetermined price.

No Obligation for Buyers

If you buy an option, you have the right to exercise it, but you are not required to do so. This means you can choose to buy or sell the underlying asset only if it is advantageous for you.

Obligation for Sellers

If you sell an option, you are obligated to fulfill the contract if the buyer decides to exercise their right. For a call option, this means delivering the underlying asset at the strike price. For a put option, it means purchasing the underlying asset at the strike price.

Expiration Period

Options are valid only for a specific period, known as the expiration period. After this period, the option expires and becomes worthless if not exercised.

Premium Payment by Buyers

When you buy an option, you pay a premium, which is a debit from your trading account. This premium is the cost of acquiring the option.

Premium Receipt by Sellers

When you sell an option, you receive a premium, which is credited to your trading account. This premium is your compensation for taking on the obligation associated with the option.

Variety of Strike Prices

Options are available at multiple strike prices, which are set levels at which the underlying asset can be bought or sold. These strike prices allow traders to choose options that align with their market outlook and trading strategies.

Chapter Summary

Chapter 1 introduces the fundamental concepts of options trading, defining an options contract as an agreement giving the buyer the right, but not the obligation, to buy or sell an asset at a specific price before the contract's expiration, with the buyer paying a premium and the seller obligated if exercised. It covers various underlying assets like stocks, indices, commodities, and currencies, and explains the uses of options for hedging, speculation, or generating income. The chapter details the different types of options (call and put), key terms (underlying asset, strike price, expiration date, premium, etc.), and important concepts like intrinsic and extrinsic values, implied volatility, and the Greeks. It emphasizes the versatility of options, their risk management potential, and the necessity of understanding these basics for successful trading.

Chapter 2

Options Trading

Understanding how options work is crucial for anyone looking to trade these versatile financial instruments. In this chapter, we will explore how options are traded, option chains, factors that affect option prices and the best uses for options.

How Options Are Traded

Options are traded on exchanges and over-the-counter (OTC) markets. Exchange-traded options are standardized contracts listed on exchanges like the Chicago Board Options Exchange (CBOE). These standardized contracts specify the details of the options, including the underlying asset, strike price, expiration date, and contract size. Trading on an exchange provides greater liquidity and transparency, as well as the assurance of standardized terms and centralized clearing.

Over-the-counter options, on the other hand, are customized contracts negotiated directly between two parties. These contracts can be tailored to meet the specific needs of the buyer and seller, offering more flexibility than exchange-traded options. However, OTC options come with higher counterparty risk, as there is no centralized clearinghouse to guarantee the fulfillment of the contract.

When trading options, investors can take various positions, such as buying calls, buying puts, selling covered calls, options spreads, and other options strategies. Each position involves a different level of risk and potential reward, and the choice of strategy depends on the investor's market outlook and risk tolerance.

Understanding Option Chains

An option chain, also known as an options matrix, is a table that displays all available options contracts for a particular underlying asset, organized by expiration date and strike price. Option chains are essential tools for options traders, as they provide a comprehensive overview of the available options and their prices.

Here are the key components of an option chain:

- Underlying Asset

- Expiration Date

- Strike Price

- Bid and Ask Prices

- Last Price

- Volume

- Open Interest

- Implied Volatility (IV)

Options chains may appear in two formats:

- **List** – As the name suggests, a list is simply a list of option contracts for a specific expiration date. Typically, these lists have descending strike prices with call options above put options.

- **Straddle** – A straddle shows calls and puts side-by-side with the strike price in the middle. Many traders prefer straddles because you can compare put versus call activity at each strike price.

Many trading platforms let you customize the variables in the option chain and show either a list or a straddle view of the options contracts for that expiration date. In our example, we are looking at the option chain for Rivian Automotive, Inc. (RIVN) in a list view. The lightly shaded area in the option chain represents options strikes that are in-the-money (ITM).

Underlying	Bid	Ask	Last	Net Change	Size	Volume	Open	High	Low
RIVN	10.05	10.06	10.06	-0.36	100x50	1,821,000	10.25	10.41	9.97

Calls

Bid	Ask	Last Price	Volume	Open Interest	IV	Expiration	Strike
1.07	1.13	1.10	8	57	72.61%	31-May-24	9.00
0.62	0.66	0.62	6	84	86.40%	31-May-24	9.50
0.26	0.29	0.30	9	169	76.40%	31-May-24	10.00
0.10	0.11	0.11	78	596	75.30%	31-May-24	10.50
0.03	0.04	0.03	226	352	88.72%	31-May-24	11.00
0.01	0.02	0.02	135	607	99.43%	31-May-24	11.50

Puts

Bid	Ask	Last Price	Volume	Open Interest	IV	Expiration	Strike
0.01	0.03	0.03	97	1907	94.55%	31-May-24	9.00
0.05	0.06	0.07	41	839	77.94%	31-May-24	9.50
0.20	0.21	0.22	75	635	76.81%	31-May-24	10.00
0.51	0.54	0.53	88	435	80.91%	31-May-24	10.50
0.94	0.99	0.97	64	242	88.09%	31-May-24	11.00
1.36	1.40	1.36	2	13	98.59%	31-May-24	11.50

By analyzing option chains, traders and investors can identify opportunities to buy or sell options based on their market outlook and risk preferences. For example, if you expect a stock's price to rise, look for call options with a favorable strike price and expiration date. Conversely, if you anticipate a decline in the stock's price, consider buying put options.

Factors that Affect Option Prices

Value of Underlying Asset

The value of the underlying asset significantly impacts the price of an options contract. For call options, as the price of the underlying asset increases, the value of the call option generally rises because the holder has the right to buy the asset at a fixed strike price. For example, if you hold a call option to buy stock at $50 and the stock's price rises to $60, the call option becomes more valuable due to the increased potential profit. Conversely, if the underlying asset's price decreases, the value of the call option tends to fall, as the likelihood of the option being profitable diminishes.

For put options, the relationship is inverse. As the price of the underlying asset decreases, the value of the put option typically increases because the holder has the right to sell the asset at a fixed strike price. For instance, if you hold a put option to sell stock at $50 and the stock's price drops to $40, the put option's value increases due to the higher potential profit. Conversely, as the underlying asset's price increases, the value of the put option tends to decrease, as the likelihood of the option being profitable diminishes.

Thus, the value of the underlying asset directly impacts the intrinsic value of both call and put options, influencing their overall market prices.

Time Decay

Time decay, also known as theta, affects the price of an options contract by eroding its value as it approaches its expiration date. This erosion impacts both call and put options and becomes more pronounced as expiration nears.

Options derive part of their value from the amount of time left until they expire, known as the extrinsic value or time value. The longer the time until expiration, the greater the time value, as there is more opportunity for the underlying asset's price to move favorably. However, as time passes, the likelihood of significant price movements decreases, leading to a gradual reduction in the option's time value.

For example, consider an option that has several months until expiration. This option will have a higher time value because there is a greater chance that the underlying asset's price will move in a way that makes the option profitable. As the option approaches its expiration date, the time value diminishes because there is less time for such movements to occur. This decrease in time value accelerates in the final weeks and days before expiration, significantly impacting the option's overall price.

Time decay affects both call and put options similarly. An option with a longer time to expiration will generally be more expensive due to the higher time value. As the expiration date approaches, the time decay accelerates, eroding the option's price even if the underlying asset's price remains stable.

Implied Volatility

Implied volatility measures the market's expectations for future price fluctuations of the underlying asset and significantly influences the price of an options contract. Unlike historical volatility, which looks at past price movements, implied volatility is forward-looking and reflects market predictions about future volatility during the option's life.

When implied volatility increases, it generally leads to higher option premiums because greater expected volatility indicates a higher likelihood of significant price movements in the underlying asset, increasing the probability that the option will end up in-the-money. For example, if a stock's implied volatility rises due to an upcoming earnings announcement, the premiums for both call and put options on that stock will increase, reflecting the market's anticipation of larger potential price swings and higher risk and potential reward for option holders.

Conversely, when implied volatility decreases, option premiums tend to fall. Lower volatility suggests that the underlying asset's price is expected to be more stable, reducing the likelihood of significant price movements and the probability of the option expiring in-the-money. Traders use implied volatility to assess the attractiveness of options; high implied volatility can indicate that options are relatively expensive, while low implied volatility can suggest they are cheaper.

Changes in implied volatility also impact the value of existing options positions, benefiting holders of long options when volatility increases and benefiting sellers of options when volatility decreases.

Liquidity

Liquidity is a critical factor affecting the price of an options contract, referring to the ease with which options can be bought or sold in the market without causing significant price changes. High liquidity is marked by many buyers and sellers, tight bid-ask spreads, and high trading volume, making it cost-effective for traders to enter and exit positions due to lower transaction costs and reduced slippage.

For example, if an options contract has high liquidity, an investor can buy or sell the option with minimal price impact and low transaction costs, which is crucial for frequent traders aiming to maximize profitability. Conversely, low liquidity means fewer market participants, resulting in wider bid-ask spreads, higher transaction costs, and greater price volatility, making it challenging to execute trades at desired prices. In low liquidity markets, large trades can significantly impact the option's price, increasing market impact costs and potentially deterring participation.

Overall, liquidity influences the attractiveness of an options contract, as highly liquid markets offer greater flexibility, lower costs, and reduced risk of price manipulation, attracting more participants and enhancing market efficiency.

Interest Rates

Interest rates significantly affect the prices of options contracts by influencing the cost of carrying an investment, known as the "cost of carry," which impacts both call and put options. The relationship between interest rates and option prices is often explained through the Black-Scholes option pricing model, which includes interest rates as a key input.

When interest rates rise, the price of call options generally increases because higher interest rates reduce the present value of the strike price, making it relatively cheaper to buy the underlying asset in the future. For instance, buying a call option allows investors to defer the purchase of the asset, and with higher interest rates, the money can be invested to earn a higher return, thus increasing the value of the option. Conversely, when interest rates rise, the price of put options generally decreases because higher interest rates increase the present value of the cash received from selling the underlying asset at the strike price. This higher opportunity cost of holding the asset rather than investing the proceeds at a higher interest rate makes holding a put option less attractive, thereby lowering its price.

For example, if interest rates rise, the time value of call options increases, making them more expensive, while the time value of put options decreases. Conversely, if interest rates fall, the time value of call options decreases, and the time value of put options increases. Thus, changes in interest rates affect the time value component of an option's premium, impacting their overall pricing and attractiveness.

Dividends

Dividends play a significant role in the pricing of options, particularly those on individual stocks. The anticipated payment of dividends can affect the prices of both call and put options. When a stock is expected to pay a dividend, the price of call options on that stock generally decreases because the stock price typically drops by approximately the dividend amount on the ex-dividend date, the first day the stock trades without the dividend.

Since call options give the holder the right to buy the stock at a specified strike price, a drop in the stock price reduces the potential profit for the call option holder. For example, if a stock is trading at $50 and is expected to pay a $2 dividend, the stock price may drop to around $48 on the ex-dividend date. This anticipated drop makes holding the call option less attractive, as the underlying asset's value is expected to decrease. As a result, the premium for call options tends to be lower when a significant dividend payment is expected.

Conversely, the expected payment of dividends generally increases the price of put options. Since put options give the holder the right to sell the stock at a specified strike price, a drop in the stock price due to the dividend payment makes the put option more valuable. The lower expected stock price increases the likelihood that the put option will be profitable. Continuing with the previous example, if the stock is expected to drop from $50 to $48 due to a $2 dividend, the put option that allows the holder to sell the stock at $50 becomes more valuable. This increased value leads to higher premiums for put options when a significant dividend payment is anticipated.

Traders and investors need to account for expected dividends when pricing options and developing trading strategies. For instance, options traders might choose to buy puts or sell calls on dividend-paying stocks to capitalize on the expected price drop. Alternatively, they might avoid holding long call positions through the ex-dividend date to prevent losses associated with the dividend-adjusted price decline. For example, an investor holding a call option on a dividend-paying stock might sell the call before the ex-dividend date to avoid the expected drop in the stock price.

Option Moneyness

Option moneyness is a crucial concept in options trading, referring to the intrinsic value of an option relative to the current price of the underlying asset. It determines whether exercising the option would be profitable at the present moment. Understanding moneyness is essential for traders because it directly impacts the value and potential profitability of an options contract. There are three primary states of moneyness: at-the-money (ATM), in-the-money (ITM), and out-of-the-money (OTM).

At-the-Money (ATM)

An option is considered at-the-money when the price of the underlying asset is exactly equal to the option's strike price. In this scenario, neither a call nor a put option has intrinsic value, but they still possess time value. For example, if a stock is trading at $50, and both the call and put options have a strike price of $50, these options are at-the-money. At-the-money options are often used by traders looking to benefit from potential price movements without having a strong directional bias. They typically have the highest time value because the likelihood of the option finishing in-the-money is at its peak.

In-the-Money (ITM)

An option is in-the-money if exercising it would result in an immediate profit. For call options, this means the underlying asset's price is above the strike price. For put options, the underlying asset's price is below the strike price. For instance, if a stock is trading at $60, a call option with a strike price of $50 is in-the-money by $10. Similarly, if the stock is trading at $40, a put option with a strike price of $50 is in-the-money by $10. In-the-money options have intrinsic value and typically command higher premiums due to their greater likelihood of being profitable at expiration.

Out-of-the-Money (OTM)

An option is out-of-the-money when exercising it would not result in a profit. For call options, this means the underlying asset's price is below the strike price, while for put options, the underlying asset's price is above the strike price. For example, if a stock is trading at $40, a call option with a strike price of $50 is out-of-the-money. Likewise, if the stock is trading at $60, a put option with a strike price of $50 is out-of-the-money. Out-of-the-money options do not have intrinsic value; they only have time value. These options are less expensive compared to in-the-money options but can still be attractive for traders expecting significant price movements in the underlying asset.

Uses of Options Contracts

Options contracts are versatile financial instruments that can be employed in various strategies to achieve different investment goals. Here are some of the primary uses of options contracts:

Hedging

Hedging is a strategy used by investors to protect against potential losses in their existing positions. By using options, investors can create a safety net for their portfolios. For example, an investor who owns a substantial number of shares in a particular stock might be concerned about a potential decline in the stock's price. To mitigate this risk, the investor can purchase put options. A put option gives the holder the right to sell the stock at a predetermined price, thus setting a floor on the potential losses. If the stock price falls below the strike price of the put option, the losses in the stock position can be offset by gains from the put option, effectively hedging against adverse price movements.

Speculation

Options are also widely used for speculation, allowing traders to bet on the direction of the market or specific assets with a relatively small investment compared to buying the underlying asset outright. Speculative traders use options to leverage their positions, aiming to profit from anticipated price movements. For instance, a trader who believes that a stock's price will rise significantly in the near future might purchase call options. If the stock price does increase, the trader can exercise the call options to buy the stock at the lower strike price or sell the options at a higher market value, achieving substantial returns on the initial investment. Conversely, if a trader expects a stock to decline, they might buy put options to profit from the anticipated drop.

Income Generation

Income generation is another common use of options contracts. Investors can earn additional income by selling options, a strategy often referred to as "writing" options. One popular income-generating strategy is writing covered calls. In this approach, an investor who owns shares of a stock sells call options on those shares. The investor collects the premium from selling the call options, providing an immediate income stream. If the stock price remains below the strike price, the options expire worthless, and the investor keeps both the premium and the shares. If the stock price rises above the strike price, the investor may have to sell the shares at the strike price, but the premium received can enhance the overall return on the investment. This strategy works well in stable or mildly bullish markets where significant price increases are not expected.

Managing Risk

In addition to hedging, options can be used in various strategies to manage risk. For example, investors can create a protective collar strategy, where they hold a long position in a stock, buy a put option to protect against downside risk, and simultaneously sell a call option to offset the cost of the put. This strategy limits both the potential loss and the potential gain, providing a balanced risk management approach.

Enhancing Returns

Advanced options strategies, such as spreads and straddles, can be used to enhance returns. These strategies involve combining multiple options contracts to capitalize on specific market conditions. For example, a trader might use a bull call spread, buying a call option at a lower strike price and selling another call option at a higher strike price. This strategy limits the potential profit but also reduces the cost compared to buying a single call option outright.

Chapter Summary

Chapter 2 provides a comprehensive exploration of options trading, beginning with an explanation of how options are traded, distinguishing between exchange-traded and over-the-counter options. It discusses various trading strategies like buying calls and puts, selling covered calls, and using options spreads, tailored to different risk profiles and market outlooks. The chapter delves into the mechanics of option chains, explaining how to read and interpret them to make informed trading decisions. It also covers critical factors influencing option prices, such as the value of the underlying asset, time decay, implied volatility, liquidity, and interest rates. The chapter concludes with practical applications of options in hedging, speculation, income generation, risk management, and enhancing returns, equipping readers with the knowledge to trade options effectively and manage risk.

Chapter 3

Basic Options Strategies

Introduction to Basic Strategies

Options trading offers a variety of strategies that can be tailored to different market conditions and investment goals. Understanding these basic strategies is essential for both novice and experienced traders to effectively manage risk and maximize returns. In this chapter, we will explore two fundamental options strategies: buying call options and buying put options. These strategies serve as the foundation for more advanced options trading techniques and provide traders with the flexibility to capitalize on market movements.

Importance of Having a Strategy

A clear strategy helps traders make informed decisions, effectively manage risk, and avoid emotional reactions to market fluctuations. Without a strategy, traders may be prone to making impulsive decisions that could lead to significant losses. A robust strategy not only outlines the conditions under which a trade will be made but also establishes criteria for exiting positions and managing potential risks. By adhering to a strategy, traders can enhance their chances of achieving consistent, long-term success in the options market.

Buying Call Options

Buying call options is a straightforward and popular strategy among traders who anticipate a rise in the price of the underlying asset.

When to Use a Long Call Strategy

The strategy of buying call options is best used when a trader expects the underlying asset's price to increase significantly within a certain timeframe. It is particularly effective in bullish market conditions or when there are positive catalysts that could drive the asset's price higher, such as strong earnings reports, favorable economic data, or industry advancements.

Potential Benefits and Risks of Call Options

The primary benefit of buying call options is the potential for significant returns with a relatively small initial investment. Since the cost of purchasing a call option (the premium) is typically much lower than buying the underlying asset outright, traders can leverage their positions to achieve higher percentage gains. Additionally, the risk for the call option buyer is limited to the premium paid for the option, providing a clear and manageable downside risk.

For example, XYZ is trading at $10 per share and you believe the stock price will go up before expiration, so you buy one contract (100 shares) of a 10 call option with an expiration that is one month out for a price of $1 ($1 x 100 shares = $100 premium). Your total risk is the premium paid, which is $100. Before the expiration, the stock goes to $12 per share and your option is now worth $2. If you sold the option at $2, you would receive $200 on an investment of $100 or 100% profit. If you had bought 100 shares of the stock at $10 per share instead, you would have still made $200 but on an investment of $1,000 ($10 x 100 shares), which is a profit of 20% but your total risk was $1000. This is the benefit of leverage.

However, there are also risks associated with buying call options. If the underlying asset's price does not increase as expected, the option may expire as worthless, resulting in a total loss of the premium paid. Moreover, time decay (theta) works against call option buyers, eroding the option's value as the expiration date approaches. Traders must accurately time their trades to ensure the underlying asset's price movement occurs within the option's lifespan.

Buying Put Options

Buying put options is a strategy employed by traders who anticipate a decline in the price of the underlying asset.

When to Use a Long Put Strategy

The strategy of buying put options is most effective when a trader expects the underlying asset's price to decrease significantly. It is particularly useful in bearish market conditions or when negative catalysts are anticipated, such as poor earnings reports, unfavorable economic data, or adverse regulatory developments.

Potential Benefits and Risks of Put Options

The primary benefit of buying put options is the ability to profit from a decline in the underlying asset's price with a limited initial investment. Similar to call options, the cost of purchasing a put option (the premium) is typically much lower than shorting the underlying asset. This allows traders to achieve substantial percentage gains if the asset's price falls. Additionally, the risk for the put option buyer is limited to the premium paid for the option, providing a clear and manageable downside risk.

For example, XYZ is trading at $10 per share and you believe the stock price will go down before expiration, so you buy one contract (100 shares) of a 10 put option with an expiration that is one month out for a price of $1 ($1 x 100 shares = $100 premium). Your total risk is the premium paid, which is $100. Before the expiration, the stock drops to $8 per share and your option is now worth $2. If you sold the option at $2, you would receive $200 on an investment of $100 or 100% profit. If you had shorted 100 shares of the stock at $10 per share instead, you would have still made $200 but your total risk would be unlimited because there is no cap on how high the stock could go. This is the benefit of risk management.

However, buying put options also comes with risks. If the underlying asset's price does not decrease as expected, the option may expire as worthless, resulting in a total loss of the premium paid. Time decay (theta) also affects put options, eroding their value as the expiration date approaches. Therefore, accurate timing is crucial for traders to capitalize on the anticipated price movement within the option's lifespan.

Chapter Summary

Chapter 3 discusses the understanding and implementing of basic options strategies like buying call options and buying put options are essential for navigating the options market. These strategies provide traders with opportunities to profit from both rising and falling markets while managing risk through limited downside exposure. As traders gain experience, they can build upon these foundational strategies to explore more complex options trading techniques.

Chapter 4

Benefits and Risks in Options Trading

Options trading offers several compelling benefits that make it an attractive choice for investors seeking to enhance their portfolios. The key advantages of options include leverage, flexibility, and risk mana-gement, each of which contributes to the unique value proposition of these financial instruments.

Leverage

One of the most significant benefits of options is leverage. Options allow investors to control a large position with a relatively small amount of capital. This means that with a modest investment, traders can gain exposure to the price movements of a much larger quantity of the underlying asset. For example, purchasing a call option gives the holder the right to buy 100 shares of a stock at a fraction of the cost of buying the shares outright. This leverage can lead to substantial returns if the underlying asset moves in the anticipated direction. However, it's important to note that while leverage can amplify gains, it can also magnify losses, making it essential for traders to carefully manage their risk.

Flexibility

Options offer unparalleled flexibility, allowing investors to design a wide range of strategies to profit from various market conditions. Whether the market is rising, falling, or remaining flat, there are options strategies that can be tailored to capitalize on these scenarios. For instance, bullish investors might buy call options to profit from an anticipated rise in stock prices, while bearish investors might buy put options to benefit from a decline. Additionally, more complex strategies like spreads, straddles, and strangles enable traders to hedge their bets and potentially profit from volatility or lack of movement in the underlying asset. This versatility makes options a powerful tool for both speculative and conservative investors.

Risk Management

Options provide valuable tools for managing risk in an investment portfolio. One of the primary uses of options is hedging, which involves taking a position in an option to offset potential losses in another investment. For example, an investor holding a long position in a stock can purchase put options to protect against a potential decline in the stock's price. This strategy, known as a protective put, ensures that the investor can sell the stock at the strike price, thus limiting their downside risk. Similarly, options can be used to lock in profits, protect against adverse market movements, and provide a measure of insurance for various investment positions. By incorporating options into their risk management strategies, investors can achieve greater stability and predictability in their portfolio performance.

Risks of Using Options

While options trading offers numerous benefits, it also comes with several inherent risks that investors need to understand and manage effectively. The primary risks associated with options include complexity, potential losses, and other factors that can impact trading outcomes.

Complexity

Options trading is inherently complex, requiring a solid understanding of various factors that influence options pricing, such as the Greeks (delta, gamma, theta, vega, and rho), volatility, and the underlying asset's price movements. Unlike straightforward stock trading, options involve multiple variables that can affect their value. This complexity necessitates a comprehensive grasp of options mechanics, pricing models like the Black-Scholes model, and the implications of different market conditions. Novice traders may find this learning curve steep and challenging, potentially leading to costly mistakes if they engage in options trading without adequate knowledge and preparation.

Potential Losses

One of the most concerning risks in options trading is the potential for significant losses, especially when selling options. While buying options limits the investor's risk to the premium paid for the option, selling options can expose the investor to unlimited losses if the market moves against their position. For example, writing (selling) naked call options, which are those not covered by an equivalent position in the underlying asset, can lead to substantial losses if the asset's price rises sharply. The seller is obligated to deliver the underlying asset at the strike price, regardless of how high the market price has risen, resulting in potentially unlimited losses. Similarly, selling put options can lead to significant losses if the asset's price plummets, as the seller must purchase the asset at the strike price, which could be far above the current market value.

Time Sensitivity

Options are time-sensitive instruments, meaning their value diminishes as they approach expiration. This phenomenon, known as time decay, can work against options buyers, eroding the option's value even if the underlying asset's price remains relatively stable. Traders must accurately time their trades to ensure that the expected price movements occur within the option's lifespan. Failure to do so can result in the option expiring worthless, leading to a total loss of the premium paid. This time sensitivity adds another layer of complexity and risk, requiring traders to not only predict price movements but also their timing.

Market Volatility

Volatility can significantly impact options prices and trading outcomes. While volatility can present opportunities for profit, it also introduces substantial risk. Implied volatility, which reflects market expectations of future volatility, can cause option premiums to fluctuate dramatically. Sudden spikes or drops in volatility can lead to unexpected changes in options prices, potentially resulting in substantial losses. Traders need to be aware of the volatility environment and adjust their strategies accordingly to manage this risk effectively.

Liquidity Risk

Liquidity risk is another important consideration in options trading. Low liquidity can lead to wider bid-ask spreads, making it more costly to enter and exit positions. In illiquid markets, traders may struggle to find counterparties to trade with at favorable prices, increasing the risk of slippage and adverse price movements. This can be particularly problematic when trying to execute large orders or complex strategies that require precise timing and pricing.

Psychological Challenges

The psychological challenges of options trading should not be underestimated. The potential for significant gains and losses can lead to emotional decision-making, such as fear and greed, which can impair judgment and result in suboptimal trading decisions. Successful options trading requires discipline, patience, and a well-defined strategy to manage emotions and stay focused on long-term objectives.

Chapter Summary

Chapter 4 explores the benefits and risks associated with options trading, highlighting its potential to enhance investment portfolios through leverage, flexibility, and risk management. Leverage allows traders to control large positions with minimal capital, offering substantial returns but also amplifying potential losses. The flexibility of options enables a variety of strategies to profit from different market conditions, such as buying calls in a bullish market or puts in a bearish one, along with more complex strategies like spreads and straddles. Options also provide valuable tools for risk management, such as hedging through protective puts to limit downside risk. However, the chapter also emphasizes the inherent risks, including the complexity of options trading, the potential for significant losses, time sensitivity due to options' expiration, market volatility, liquidity risks, and psychological challenges. Understanding these risks and developing effective strategies to manage them are essential for successful options trading.

Chapter 5

Practical Tips for Successful Options Trading

Setting Up Your Trading Plan

Setting up a robust trading plan is a critical first step towards successful options trading. A trading plan serves as a roadmap, guiding you through the complexities of the market and helping you make informed decisions based on predefined criteria rather than emotions. It is essential to have a clear and structured plan that outlines your objectives, strategies, risk management protocols, and performance evaluation methods. This discipline can significantly improve your chances of achieving consistent success in options trading.

Importance of a Trading Plan

The importance of a trading plan cannot be overstated. It provides a structured approach to trading, ensuring that your decisions are driven by logic and strategy rather than impulsive reactions to market movements. A well-crafted trading plan helps you stay focused on your goals, manage risk effectively, and avoid common pitfalls that can derail your trading efforts.

Additionally, a trading plan can help you maintain discipline, stick to your strategy, and manage emotions such as fear and greed that often lead to poor decision-making.

Elements of a Good Trading Plan

A good trading plan should include the following key elements:

Clear Objectives

Define what you want to achieve with your trading. Are you looking to generate regular income, grow your capital, or hedge against other investments? Having clear objectives helps you tailor your strategies to meet your specific goals.

Strategy Outline

Detail the specific strategies you plan to use, such as buying calls or puts, writing covered calls, or using spreads. Include criteria for entering and exiting trades, such as technical indicators, fundamental analysis, or market conditions.

Risk Management

Establish rules for managing risk, including position sizing, stop-loss orders, and diversification. Determine the maximum amount of capital you are willing to risk on a single trade and ensure you have measures in place to protect your portfolio from significant losses.

Performance Evaluation

Set up a system for tracking and evaluating your trading performance. Keep detailed records of your trades, including the rationale behind each trade, entry and exit points, and outcomes. Regularly review your performance to identify strengths and weaknesses and make necessary adjustments to your plan.

Contingency Plans

Prepare for unexpected market events or changes in your personal circumstances. Have a plan in place for handling market volatility, liquidity issues, or other unforeseen challenges that may arise.

Common Mistakes to Avoid

Avoiding common mistakes is crucial for both novice and experienced traders. Here are some common pitfalls and how to avoid them:

Lack of Preparation

Many traders enter the market without sufficient knowledge or preparation. Take the time to educate yourself about options trading, understand the mechanics of the strategies you plan to use, and stay informed about market conditions.

Overleveraging

Using excessive leverage can amplify both gains and losses. Avoid risking too much of your capital on a single trade and ensure your position sizes are appropriate for your risk tolerance and overall portfolio size.

Ignoring Risk Management

Failing to implement proper risk management techniques can lead to significant losses. Always use stop-loss orders, diversify your positions, and adhere to your risk management rules.

Emotional Trading

Allowing emotions to drive your trading decisions can result in impulsive actions and poor outcomes. Stick to your trading plan, maintain discipline, and avoid making decisions based on fear or greed.

Chasing Losses

Trying to recover losses by taking increasingly risky trades can exacerbate your financial situation. Accept that losses are a part of trading, learn from them, and move on without deviating from your strategy.

Learning from Unsuccessful Trades

Learning from unsuccessful trades is an integral part of becoming a successful options trader. Each loss provides an opportunity to gain valuable insights and improve your trading approach. Here are some steps to help you learn from your mistakes:

Analyze Your Trades

After each trade, analyze the outcome and identify what went right and what went wrong. Look for patterns in your trading behavior that may be contributing to your losses.

Keep a Trading Journal

Maintain a detailed trading journal that documents every trade, including the rationale behind it, the strategy used, and the results. Reviewing your journal regularly can help you identify areas for improvement and reinforce positive habits.

Adjust Your Plan

Use the insights gained from your analysis to refine your trading plan. Make adjustments to your strategies, risk management rules, or performance evaluation methods as needed to enhance your overall trading approach.

Seek Feedback

Engage with other traders, mentors, or trading communities to gain different perspectives on your trades. Constructive feedback can provide new ideas and help you avoid repeating the same mistakes.

Stay Committed to Learning

Options trading is a continuous learning process. Stay committed to improving your skills, expanding your knowledge, and adapting to changing market conditions. By embracing a mindset of continuous improvement, you can turn unsuccessful trades into valuable learning experiences that contribute to your long-term success.

Chapter Summary

Chapter 5 equips traders with practical strategies and essential insights for success in options trading, emphasizing the importance of a robust trading plan that includes clear objectives, detailed strategies, risk management protocols, and performance evaluation methods. It highlights common mistakes to avoid, such as lack of preparation, overleveraging, ignoring risk management, emotional trading, and chasing losses, and underscores the critical role of continuous learning through maintaining a trading journal, analyzing trades, seeking feedback, and refining the trading plan. By following these guidelines, traders can navigate the options market more confidently and work towards achieving their financial goals.

Closing Points

The Road Ahead

Recap of Key Points

In this book, "Options Trading Basics: A Beginner's Guide to Understanding Options," we've covered the essential aspects of options trading to equip you with the knowledge and skills needed to navigate this complex financial instrument. Let's briefly recap the key points from each chapter.

In Chapter 1: Understanding Options, we explored the fundamental concepts of options contracts, including the definitions, types of options (calls and puts), and essential terms such as strike price, expiration date, and premium. We also discussed the different exercise styles, intrinsic and extrinsic values, implied volatility, and the Greeks.

Chapter 2: How Options Work detailed the mechanics of options trading. We explained how options are traded on exchanges and over-the-counter markets, the components of an options chain, and the factors that influence options prices, including the value of the underlying asset, time decay, implied volatility, liquidity, interest rates, and dividends.

In Chapter 3: Basic Options Strategies, we introduced fundamental strategies like buying call options and buying put options. We discussed when to use these strategies, their potential benefits and risks, and provided examples to illustrate how these strategies work in practice.

Chapter 4: Benefits and Risks in Options Trading highlighted the advantages of options, such as leverage, flexibility, and risk management, while also addressing the inherent risks like complexity, potential losses, time sensitivity, market volatility, liquidity risk, and psychological challenges. This balanced perspective helps in making informed decisions about options trading.

Finally, Chapter 5: Practical Tips for Successful Options Trading offered insights into setting up a trading plan, avoiding common mistakes, and learning from unsuccessful trades. Emphasizing the importance of discipline, preparation, and continuous learning, this chapter provides practical advice for achieving long-term success in options trading.

The Importance of Continued Education

While this book has provided a comprehensive introduction to options trading, the world of options is vast and ever evolving. Continuous education is crucial to staying ahead and making informed decisions. Markets change, new strategies emerge, and your personal financial goals may evolve over time. By committing to ongoing learning, you can adapt to these changes and refine your trading skills.

Engage with advanced resources, participate in trading forums, and seek mentorship to deepen your understanding. Stay updated on market trends, economic indicators, and regulatory changes that may impact your trading strategies. The more knowledge you accumulate, the better equipped you will be to navigate the complexities of options trading and capitalize on new opportunities.

Final Thoughts

Options trading offers a powerful toolset for enhancing your investment portfolio through leverage, risk management, and strategic flexibility. By applying the knowledge and strategies discussed in this book, you can take the first steps towards becoming a confident and successful options trader.

Remember, the key to mastering options trading lies in continuous practice, disciplined risk management, and a commitment to learning. Use the concepts and techniques you've learned here as a foundation and build upon them as you gain experience and deepen your understanding.

Thank you for embarking on this journey with "Options Trading Basics: A Beginner's Guide to Understanding Options." We hope this book has provided you with valuable insights and practical tools to help you succeed in the options market. Now, it's time to apply what you've learned and explore the exciting opportunities that options trading can offer. Good luck and happy trading!

Thank You for Reading!

We hope you found "*Options Trading Basics: A Beginner's Guide to Understanding Options*" valuable and insightful. Your book review is incredibly important to us and helps other readers discover the benefits of this book.

Share Your Thoughts

If you enjoyed this book and found it helpful, we would greatly appreciate it if you could take a few moments to leave a review on Amazon. Your review will provide valuable insights for other readers and help us with our future publications.

How to Leave a Review

1. **Visit the Amazon Page:**

   o Go to the product page for "**Options Trading Basics: A Beginner's Guide to Understanding Options**" on Amazon.

2. **Sign In to Your Account:**

   o Make sure you are logged into your Amazon account.

3. **Leave Your Review:**

   o Scroll down to the "Customer Reviews" section.

   o Click on the "Write a customer review" button.

   o Share your thoughts about the book. Mention what you found most helpful or interesting.

We Value Your Feedback

Your feedback not only helps other potential readers but also assists us in enhancing our content to better serve you.

Connect with Us

If you have any further comments or would like to share your thoughts directly, feel free to reach out to me at....

mjdefosse@marketsavvyinvestor.com.

Thank you for your support and happy trading!

Sincerely,

Michael J. Defosse, MS, MBA

www.ingramcontent.com/pod-product-compliance
Lightning Source LLC
Chambersburg PA
CBHW070135230526
45472CB00004B/1532